Guess Who
Hides

Sharon Gordon

BENCHMARK BOOKS

MARSHALL CAVENDISH
NEW YORK

Splash!

I go into the pond.

It is too hot to sit in the sun.

I swim to the muddy bottom.

I find my favorite food here.

I eat plants, insects, and fish.

I also eat dead animals.

This helps keep the
pond clean.

I have large eyes to see.

I do not have teeth.

I do not need any.

I can bite hard with my jaw.

I lay my eggs in the sand.

I dig a hole with my back legs.

The eggs hatch in about 60 days.

The *hatchlings* hurry to the water.

I do not have bones inside my body.

I have a hard shell on the outside.

My shell is my home.

It is a great place to hide.

I pull in my arms, legs, and head.

Try to get me now!

My shell is heavy.

I move slowly.

Who am I?

I am a turtle!

Who am I?

egg

eye

hatchling

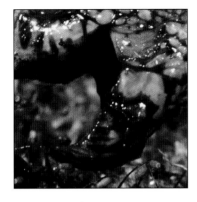

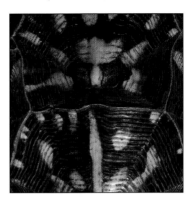

jaw   **shell**

Challenge Word

hatchling (hach-ling)

A baby turtle that has just hatched, or broken out of its egg.

Index

Page numbers in **boldface** are illustrations.

About the Author

Sharon Gordon has written many books for young children. She has also worked as an editor. Sharon and her husband Bruce have three children, Douglas, Katie, and Laura, and one spoiled pooch, Samantha. They live in Midland Park, New Jersey.

With thanks to Nanci Vargus, Ed.D. and
Beth Walker Gambro, reading consultants

Benchmark Books
Marshall Cavendish
99 White Plains Road
Tarrytown, New York 10591-9001
www.marshallcavendish.com

Library of Congress Cataloging-in-Publication Data

Gordon, Sharon.
Guess who hides / Sharon Gordon.
p. cm. — (Bookworms: Guess who)
Includes index.
Summary: Clues about the turtle's physical characteristics, behavior,
and habitat lead the reader to guess what animal is being described.
ISBN 0-7614-1555-6
1. Turtles—Juvenile literature. [1. Turtles.] I. Title.
II. Series: Gordon, Sharon. Bookworms: Guess who.

QL666.C5G67 2003
597.92—dc21
2002155813

Photo Research by Anne Burns Images

Cover Photo by: *Corbis*/Joe McDonald

The photographs in this book are used with the permission and through the courtesy of: *Corbis*: pp. 1, 23, 27 Lynda Richardson;
p. 5 Corbis; pp. 11, 15, 25, 28 (upper left and right) Joe McDonald; pp. 13, 29 (left) David Northcott;
pp. 19, 29 (right) Mary Ann McDonald; p. 21 Gary Carter. *Animals, Animals*: p. 3 E.R. Degginger. *Visuals Unlimited*:
p. 7 Jim Merli; p. 9 Warren Stone; pp. 17, 30 (lower) Joe McDonald.

Series design by Becky Terhune

Printed in China
1   3   5   6   4   2